WORLD ALMANAC® LIBRARY
OF THE
AMERICAN REVOLUTION

Forming a New American Government

Dale Anderson

WORLD ALMANAC® LIBRARY

Please visit our web site at: www.worldalmanaclibrary.com
For a free color catalog describing World Almanac® Library's list of high-quality books
and multimedia programs, call 1-800-848-2928 (USA) or 1-800-387-3178 (Canada).
World Almanac® Library's fax: (414) 332-3567.

Library of Congress Cataloging-in-Publication Data

Anderson, Dale, 1953–
     Forming a new American government / by Dale Anderson.
          p. cm. — (World Almanac Library of the American Revolution)
     Includes bibliographical references and index.
     ISBN 0-8368-5932-4 (lib. bdg.)
     ISBN 0-8368-5941-3 (softcover)
     1. United States—Politics and government—1783-1809—Juvenile literature. 2. United States—
Politics and government—1775-1783—Juvenile literature. I. Title. II. Series.
     E302.1.A53   2005
     973.4—dc22   2005040814

First published in 2006 by
World Almanac® Library
A Member of the WRC Media Family of Companies
330 West Olive Street, Suite 100
Milwaukee, WI 53212 USA

Copyright © 2006 by World Almanac® Library.

Produced by Discovery Books
Editor: Sabrina Crewe
Designer and page production: Sabine Beaupré
Photo researcher: Sabrina Crewe
Maps and diagrams: Stefan Chabluk
Consultant: Andrew Frank, Assistant Professor of History, Florida Atlantic University
World Almanac® Library editorial direction: Mark J. Sachner
World Almanac® Library editor: Alan Wachtel
World Almanac® Library art direction: Tammy West
World Almanac® Library production: Jessica Morris

Photo credits: CORBIS: pp. 8, 9, 14, 30; The Granger Collection: cover, pp. 21, 22; Independence National Historical Park:
title page, pp. 7, 11, 16, 36; National Archives: pp. 10, 20, 31, 40, 43; North Wind Picture Archives: pp. 5, 13, 15, 19, 25, 26,
28, 33, 34, 37, 39, 41.

Printed in Canada

1 2 3 4 5 6 7 8 9 09 08 07 06 05

*Front cover: George Washington (standing right, on platform), hero of the American Revolution and soon to be first
U.S. president, presides over the Constitutional Convention in 1787. Delegates came to the convention to create a
new framework of government for the United States of America.*

*Title page: James Peale painted this portrait of George Washington on horseback in about 1790. He based the
portrait on a work by his brother, Charles Willson Peale—the faces of both the brothers can be seen on the left,
behind Washington. In the background on the right are Revolutionary soldiers, one carrying a French flag.*

Contents

I n 1776, the thirteen British **colonies** along the eastern coast of North America declared themselves independent of Britain. The colonists were already fighting British soldiers in protest at British policies. In 1781, the British surrendered to American forces, and, in 1783, they formally recognized the colonies' independence.

A New Nation

The movement from colonies to independence, known as the American Revolution, gave birth to a new nation—the United States of America. Eventually, the nation stretched to the Pacific Ocean and grew to comprise fifty states. Over time, it was transformed from a nation of farmers into an industrial and technological giant, the world's richest and most powerful country.

An Inspiration to Others

The American Revolution was based on a revolution of ideas. The people who led the American Revolution believed that the purpose of government was to serve the people, not the reverse. They rejected rule by monarchs and created in its place a **republic**. The founders of the republic later wrote a **constitution** that set up this form of government and guaranteed people's basic rights, including the right to speak their minds and the freedom to worship as they wished.

The ideals on which the United States of America was founded have inspired people all around the world ever since. Within a few years of the American Revolution, the people of France had risen up against their monarchy. Over time, the people of colonies in Central

*In the early days of the American Revolution, Patriot leaders gathered in the Continental **Congress** to make decisions. In July 1776, they made their most important decision: to declare independence. This picture shows members of the Congress signing the Declaration of Independence.*

and South America, in Asia, and in Africa followed the U.S. example and rebelled against their position as colonists. Many former colonies have become independent nations.

Creating a Government

The **Patriots** who led the American Revolution from 1775 faced two tasks. They had to win the war to make their independence a reality. They also had to form a new government that could preserve that independence.

In confronting the second challenge, the new nation's leaders tried to balance several goals. They believed that government power, if unchecked, produced tyranny. Thus, they wanted to limit government to protect the rights of each citizen. They believed that government was based on the consent of the people, and they insisted on an elected government. At the same time, many leaders, including men of property, feared that too much **democracy** might lead to laws that took away wealth, privilege, and the right to own slaves. To prevent the tyranny of the majority, they wanted checks on how much power people had. Finally, leaders wanted to maintain independence for each state while also having a strong enough national government. These goals shaped the debates and compromises that marked the creation of a **federal** government.

CHAPTER ONE

New Forms of Government

One other belief drove American leaders in their efforts to form a new government. The British constitution, under which the colonies had been ruled for so long, was a combination of laws, agreements, and traditions. The Americans believed that the lack of a formal framework of government had allowed the British government to abuse its power. They firmly believed that they had to create written documents that spelled out the powers of government in the United States—and the limits to those powers.

What Was the Congress?

The Second Continental Congress met from May 10, 1775, almost continuously to 1781. It was a somewhat fluid group, with differing numbers of **delegates** from each state. In fact, in its first session, one state—Georgia—had no official representative.

Early on, the people who served in the Continental Congress knew that they had no formally granted powers. When they began meeting, America was still a set of British colonies, and there was nothing in the British colonial system to allow for a body like the Congress, which existed in opposition to the British system of colonial government. The delegates were sent by

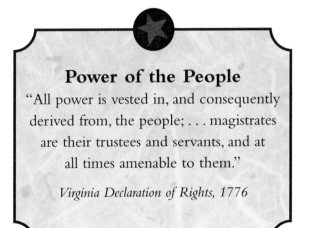

The Congress met in this building in Philadelphia during the American Revolution. Originally the State House of the Province of Pennsylvania, the building is now called Independence Hall.

self-appointed leaders in each colony. In fact, the colonies—soon to be called states—had no elected governments either. The Patriots in each colony and in the Congress all claimed to be voicing the views of the majority of Americans, but they had no way of knowing whether that was indeed true.

Creating State Governments

From the beginning, however, the Patriots sought to establish representative government. As early as the spring of 1776, the Congress voted to urge Patriots in each colony to write new constitutions so that they could create official, elected governments. They also formed a committee to draw up a plan of government for the colonies as a whole.

Two former colonies created new state governments with little effort. Both Rhode Island and Connecticut had royal **charters** dating from the 1600s. The charters had set up gov-

ernments that essentially allowed the people of those colonies to govern themselves. Connecticut and Rhode Island simply deleted all mention of Britain and the king from the charters and used them as state constitutions.

Writing State Constitutions

Several former colonies finished writing their constitutions within months. These state governments varied, but they all placed limits on

7

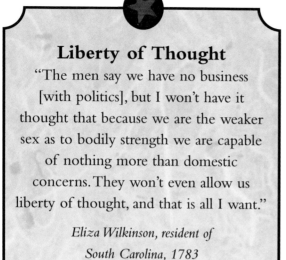

Liberty of Thought

"The men say we have no business [with politics], but I won't have it thought that because we are the weaker sex as to bodily strength we are capable of nothing more than domestic concerns. They won't even allow us liberty of thought, and that is all I want."

Eliza Wilkinson, resident of South Carolina, 1783

Most of the constitutions said that only white, male property owners could vote. This included the majority of white males, but it cut out some poorer workers. And the states denied voting rights to African Americans, Native Americans, and women.

The New Legislatures

Most of the new state governments had two houses in their **legislatures**. The larger of the two was more directly responsive to the people and supposed to reflect their wishes. In many states, its members were elected each year, and limits were set on the number of terms a person could serve. The smaller chamber was supposed to be filled by the most

the power of governors. In the past, governors had been appointed by the British king and had ultimate control over their colonies. Pennsylvania abolished the governor's office altogether.

For a while, American women could vote in the state of New Jersey, as shown here, but they had to be women who owned property above a certain value. The state took women's voting rights away in 1807.

influential people of the state, who would use their position to tone down any **radical** ideas that developed in the larger house. Two states —Pennsylvania and Georgia—had just a single legislative house.

Giving a Voice to the People

The new state governments were fairly democratic in two ways. First, colonial legislatures had for years been dominated by the older communities along the coast. People living on the western

Slavery in State Laws

Slaves could be found in every one of the British colonies at the time they became states. Many delegates to the Continental Congress owned slaves, and others profited from the slave trade or from goods produced by slave labor. In their fight for freedom and individual rights, one of the rights they wanted was the right to own slaves. Some people, however, were bothered by the contradiction between Patriot ideals and the presence of slavery. None of the new state constitutions banned slavery, but some states later took steps to do so. In

A 1784 advertisement offers slaves for sale.

1780, Pennsylvania's legislature passed a law calling for slaves to be freed over time. Three years later, the Massachusetts Supreme Court ruled that slavery violated the state's **bill of rights**. Even some southern states acted to limit slavery. Virginia and North Carolina joined with northern states in banning the importation of slaves from Africa.

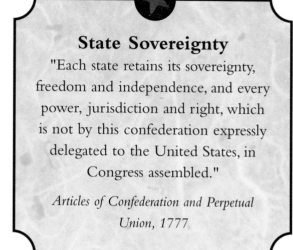

The Articles of Confederation served as the United States' first constitution. They declared that the states had entered into "a firm league of friendship with each other." This is the corrected document that was approved in November 1777.

State Sovereignty

"Each state retains its sovereignty, freedom and independence, and every power, jurisdiction and right, which is not by this confederation expressly delegated to the United States, in Congress assembled."

Articles of Confederation and Perpetual Union, 1777

In just a few years, several states found their new governments ineffective. Without a strong governor, it was hard to make sure laws were properly executed. Many revised their constitutions to increase the power of the governor. Pennsylvania, which had eliminated the office, reinstated it and gave the governor the power of **veto**.

The Articles of Confederation

The task of writing a framework for the national government, meanwhile, was given to Pennsylvania's John Dickinson. He delivered his draft on July 12, 1776. It was called the "Articles of Confederation and Perpetual Union."

Dickinson's national government, like the Continental Congress, consisted of only a legislature made up of representatives from each state. The government had no national executive officer, such as a president,

frontiers of the colonies had little voice in their colonies' laws. The new state constitutions, however, gave western settlers better representation in the new legislatures. Second, six constitutions included clear statements of the fundamental freedoms to which all citizens were entitled. This was an important step toward equal rights.

and no courts of law. Each state had one vote in the Congress. Basic decisions required a simple majority of seven states. More important decisions, such as a declaration of war, needed nine states' approval. Any changes to the Articles themselves required the approval of all thirteen states in the Congress *and* the approval of all thirteen state legislatures.

Approving the Articles

The Congress did not approve the Articles of Confederation right away. Carrying on the war remained a higher priority. In November 1777, it finally passed them and sent the document to the states for their approval. The final version had some changes from the original. Most important was the clause that allowed individual states—not the Congress, as Dickinson had preferred—control of lands west of the original colonies. This land was claimed by specific states, and some of the claims were conflicting.

The claims proved a sticking point. Some states without western claims resented this clause, believing the land should be shared. Maryland held up the Articles by refusing to give its approval unless the states with western claims gave control of those lands to the national government. When that finally happened, Maryland approved the Articles. On March 1, 1781, the Congress declared that the Articles of Confederation were in effect.

John Dickinson (1732–1808)

John Dickinson—one of the leading figures of the Continental Congress—was a highly respected lawyer and writer. With land in both Delaware and Pennsylvania, he was also very wealthy. Throughout 1775 and 1776, Dickinson urged caution and encouraged efforts to make peace. Soon after independence was approved, however, he left the Congress to join the **militia**, serving until 1778. Dickinson later served in the Congress and in the state governments of Pennsylvania and Delaware. In the 1780s, Dickinson helped found the college in Carlisle, Pennsylvania, that bears his name.

CHAPTER TWO

The Congress at War

The legislature that succeeded the Second Continental Congress under the Articles of Confederation was the Confederation Congress. Continuing the work of the Continental Congress, it operated from March 2, 1781, to late in 1788. During the war, the Congress continued to meet in Philadelphia, although British movements forced the delegates to flee on occasion to other cities. After the war, the Congress met sometimes in New Jersey and Maryland but mostly in New York City.

Congressional Members

Under the Articles of Confederation, each state sent between two and seven delegates to the Congress each year. Members could serve more than one term, but not more than three years out of any six. More than fifty men elected to the Congress never attended. Some were reluctant to leave home and preferred to concentrate on state government. Others were serving in the military.

Limited Powers

The main powers of the Confederation Congress lay in foreign affairs. It had the power to declare war and make **treaties**. The Congress's powers, however, were sharply limited. The state legislatures controlled many key decisions. For instance, the Congress could raise an army, but it had to ask the states to supply the soldiers. Similarly, it could raise money to carry out the war but had no power to impose **taxes**. All the Congress could do was request money from the states. The state legislatures—directly elected by the people— were seen as the people's true representatives.

Delegates at War

More than one-third of the 340 men elected to the Congress during the war years served for a time in either the Continental army or the militia. Several were wounded, and several were captured. Many of those who did not fight themselves lost their sons in the war. The son of Henry Laurens of South Carolina was killed in a skirmish that took place nearly a year after the Battle of Yorktown brought an end to the main fighting. Laurens received the news while serving on the commission that negotiated the treaty to end the war.

George Washington (left) and Alexander Hamilton (right) met while serving in the Continental army during the American Revolution. Both men later played important roles in the nation's government, Washington as president and Hamilton as secretary of the Treasury.

Treaties and Alliances

"The United States in Congress assembled shall have the sole and exclusive right and power of determining on peace and war, . . . of sending and receiving ambassadors—[and of] entering into treaties and alliances . . ."

Article IX, Articles of Confederation, 1777

The Congress and Its Committees

An officer called the president led sessions of the Confederation Congress. This person was not like the president today—he simply called meetings into session and maintained order.

Much of the work done by the Continental Congress had taken place in committees, and the Confederation Congress continued to work that way.

This drawing shows the Continental army on the march. During the American Revolution, soldiers often went without pay because the Congress simply had no money.

The Committee of Commerce, for instance, had the job of obtaining war supplies. The Marine Committee oversaw the Continental navy.

The Board of War had been formed by the Continental Congress in 1776 to oversee the army. In 1777, some members of the Congress tried to use the board to remove George Washington from command of the army. That effort collapsed in early 1778, and Washington remained in charge. Still, the Congress continued to interfere with its commander-in-chief. A notable example was its choice of General Horatio Gates to lead the fight against the British in the South in 1780—a choice that ended in Gates's failure and disgrace.

Several committees carried over from wartime to peacetime. The Committee of Secret Correspondence was formed in 1775 to communicate with people in Britain friendly to the American cause. It later became the part of the Congress that handled foreign relations. In 1781, the Congress replaced the committee with a single person, the secretary of foreign affairs.

Raising Money

One of the Congress's most important tasks was raising the money needed to carry on the war. This job was made difficult by the fact that the Congress had no power to collect taxes. The Congress had only three ways of raising money—borrowing money, printing it, or begging the states for it.

The Congress did all three. The states provided some funds, but never as much as the Congress requested. Rich individuals and foreign nations loaned money to the United States. The main source of funding was the paper money that the Congress issued

This drawing shows a collection of Continental bills from different years and for varying sums. The Congress issued Continental dollars that it used for funds to pay for the war against the British. Once the money was in circulation, however, it soon lost its value.

in the form of Continental dollars. Since the Congress had little gold to back the currency, however, the money lost value. By 1777, a Continental dollar was only worth 33 cents in gold. Two years later, its value had fallen to just 10 cents.

Empty Treasury

The financial crisis became clear in 1781, around the time of the decisive Battle of Yorktown, in Virginia. On their way to fight in Virginia, the Continental army passed through Philadelphia, where the Congress was based. The troops demanded to be paid. Congress members had to scramble to borrow enough money in coins to give the soldiers a month's pay. Soon after, when the battle had been won, a courier raced from Virginia to Philadelphia with news of the victory. The messenger expected to have his expenses paid, as was customary, but

Robert Morris (1734–1806)

Born in England, Robert Morris came to America in his teens. He immediately began working in the Philadelphia business of merchant Charles Willing and soon became a partner in the firm. Morris's company grew to be one of the leading trading companies in America. Morris joined the Patriot cause when war broke out. He borrowed money to finance the Revolution and lent his own money to fund the army when things were desperate. In the last years of the Revolution, the Congress appointed Morris as superintendent of finance. In 1784, Morris tired of the pressures of the job and resigned. After the war, he served in the U.S. Senate. In the 1790s, his business affairs collapsed, and he lost his fortune. Morris spent more than three years in prison for failure to repay debts. After his release, he lived the rest of his life in obscurity.

the national treasury was empty. Several members of the Congress again had to reach into their pockets to come up with the needed cash.

Morris Takes Charge

By this time, the country's finances were in a shambles. People refused to accept the paper money. In desperation, the Congress asked the states to buy the paper money at a discounted value. It also named Pennsylvania's Robert Morris as the superintendent of finance. Morris took several steps in an effort to get needed gold into the nation's treasury. The most successful tactic was to obtain more loans from European countries.

Morris also tried to convince the states to agree to a tax on **imports**. Several approved the plan, but Rhode Island refused. Without **unanimous** consent from the states, the tax could not take effect. In 1783, Morris again argued for the tax. This time, New York turned the plan down.

Officers Demand Payment

Money disputes led to a crisis in the war's last years. The Congress had, at Washington's urging, promised to pay army officers' expenses during the war and to pay them a pension afterward. In the spring of 1783, everyone knew that a peace treaty with Britain would soon be finalized, and the army would be disbanded. But the Congress had

Resisting Civil Discord

"In the name of our common country, as you value your own sacred honor, as you respect the right of humanity, and as you regard the military and national character of America, . . . express your utmost horror and detestation of the man who wishes, under any specious pretences, to overturn the liberties of our country, and who wickedly attempts to open the flood gates of civil discord, and deluge our rising empire in blood."

George Washington, speech to officers at Newburgh, New York, 1783

not yet taken steps to meet those promises to the officers. A few members of the Congress hoped to provoke a crisis with the officers so the states would be convinced to grant the Congress the power to tax. They secretly urged officers to protest. Some officers began circulating a statement that threatened a challenge to the government if their demands were not met.

Washington stepped in to defuse the situation. He called a meeting of officers and made a passionate speech about the dangers of a civil war. With that, the rebellion fizzled out. A week later, the Congress voted to give army officers a payment of a lump sum equal to five years' pay.

CHAPTER THREE

The Postwar Congress

The Congress faced many difficulties during the war. While it could not solve the country's financial mess, the government accomplished a great deal. It created an army and chose a commander in chief and other officers. Its representatives in Europe obtained vital aid. It signed a treaty with France that helped achieve American victory and another with Britain that established independence. Above all, it promoted the creation of state legislatures and, in writing the Articles of Confederation, created the first American national government. It remained to be seen how that government would perform, however, when the Revolution was over.

Organizing Territories

One of the first issues the Congress faced after the war was how to deal with the lands west of the Appalachian Mountains. The Congress hoped to organize the areas into **territories** and then raise money by selling the land to settlers. Some settlers were already there, and the Congress forced them to pay it for their lands so they could stay.

The State of Franklin

Not everyone wanted to be part of the territories proposed by the Congress. The area that is now Tennessee had originally belonged to North Carolina. In 1784, North Carolina gave control of this area to the national government. The people in eastern Tennessee banded together and formed their own government for a state they named Franklin, after Benjamin Franklin. The Congress, however, refused to recognize this rebel state.

After the American Revolution, settlers from the eastern states headed into western territories to claim land.

When North Carolina tried to reassert control over the area, fights broke out between the two sides. In 1790, the United States designated the area part of the Southwest Territory. Six years later, what was once the state of Franklin was admitted into the Union as part of the state of Tennessee.

Splitting the Northwest

The Confederation Congress enjoyed one of its greatest successes in the area north of the Ohio River and around the Great Lakes, known as the Northwest. In May of 1785, the Congress passed a law setting forth how the land in the area would be sold. The entire region would be measured and divided into areas of

36 square miles (93 square kilometers) called townships. Those would be split further into thirty-six sections of 1 square mile (2.59 sq km) each.

In the end, much of the land was sold cheaply to land **speculators**. The Congress granted huge tracts of land to two companies that could then

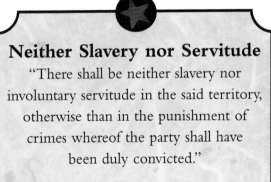

Neither Slavery nor Servitude

"There shall be neither slavery nor involuntary servitude in the said territory, otherwise than in the punishment of crimes whereof the party shall have been duly convicted."

Northwest Ordinance, 1787

divide the land into smaller pieces to sell—at higher prices—to people who wanted to settle and farm the land.

The Northwest Ordinance

Two years later, the Congress passed the Northwest **Ordinance** of 1787. The law set rules for creating states in the Northwest. It said the area would be split into three to five territories, each of which could eventually become a state with the same rights and powers as the original states.

Loans and Taxes

Back in the East, meanwhile, people were in the midst of hard economic times. Many merchants and large landowners had lent money to the government during the war. They

The Northwest Ordinance introduced an important principle: the United States could grow, and any states that joined later would be equal to the original thirteen. The law also banned slavery in western lands.

American soldiers defeat Miami warriors in the Battle of Fallen Timbers of 1794.

Native American Lands

The Congress's plans for the Northwest came up against a difficult reality—Native Americans still lived there. The Indians of the Great Lakes region had been outraged when the British gave that land away in the 1783 treaty ending the American Revolution. Native American leaders, reported one British officer, were shocked that the British king "could pretend to cede to America what was not his own to give."

The American government signed treaties with several tribes in which the Native Americans agreed to give up their lands, but others refused to do so. Violence erupted from time to time. Little Turtle, a leader of the Miami people, won two battles against white forces in present-day Ohio. In 1794, however, a larger American army under General Anthony Wayne defeated the Miami in the Battle of Fallen Timbers. The next year, the Miami gave up huge chunks of land in the Treaty of Greenville. A similar story occurred south of the Ohio River. Whites and Native Americans fought several times, and in the end the Cherokee people—one of the largest tribes in the area—were forced to give up some of their land. They were allowed to remain in parts of present-day northwestern Georgia and northeastern Alabama.

The farmers of Shays' Rebellion were fired on by militia when they tried to take over the arsenal at Springfield, Massachusetts, in 1787. The rebellion failed, but it did make government leaders pay attention to the plight of the farmers.

persuaded state legislatures to pass tax laws that would generate the revenue needed to pay off their loans. The taxes, however, fell on farmers who had little cash to pay them. When the farmers could not pay their taxes, local sheriffs seized their land and threw the farmers in jail.

Shays' Rebellion

In late 1786, some Massachusetts farmers rebelled against the land seizures. Under the leadership of former Continental army officer Daniel Shays, about 2,500 of them, many wearing their Continental army uniforms, gathered with guns in hand and marched on county courthouses to shut down the courts. This action was known as Shays' Rebellion.

State leaders denounced the revolt and organized a militia to end it. In January 1787, that army met the farmers. A few of the rebels were killed or wounded, and hundreds were arrested.

The Massachusetts state legislature also passed a law stripping the rebels of their right to vote or hold office. Even former revolutionaries, such as Samuel Adams, backed the government's steps to put down Shays' Rebellion.

Scarcity of Cash

"In almost all parts of the country, the people experience a scarcity of cash unknown in any former period. The jails [are] crowded with debtors, who find it impossible to raise money to pay their debts."

Massachusetts Centinel, *1785*

Enemies of the Revolution

"Those men, who . . . would lessen the weight of government lawfully exercised must be enemies to our happy Revolution and common liberty."

Former Patriot leader Samuel Adams, 1786

Meeting in Maryland

Shays' Rebellion was the most extreme of the popular risings against the Confederation Congress. Concern over this unrest came at the same time that some leaders were worrying about the country's growing financial crisis.

In 1786—before Shays' Rebellion —James Madison of Virginia convinced his legislature to propose a meeting to talk about trade policy. Madison hoped to persuade people to allow the Congress to tax imported goods, thereby generating much needed income for the government.

The meeting took place in Annapolis, Maryland, in September 1786. Leaders came from only five states, clearly not enough to change national policy about trade. But Alexander Hamilton of New York suggested that they call on all the states to come to another meeting, in Philadelphia in May 1787, to discuss not just trade problems but possible reform of the national government. The Congress gave its approval.

Daniel Shays (c. 1747–1825)

Daniel Shays was an ordinary farmer and Revolutionary War veteran when he became one of several leaders of the farmers' rebellion of 1786 and 1787. Few records of Shays' early life exist. He joined the militia at the Battle of Lexington and Concord and also fought at Bunker Hill, Saratoga, and Stony Point. Well regarded both by his men and his superior officers, Shays became a captain in the Continental army. The Marquis de Lafayette, one of Washington's generals, gave Shays a sword as a gift, but Shays was so poor after the war that he was forced to sell it. Shays was condemned to death for his part in the farmers' revolt, but the Massachusetts Supreme Court later lifted the death sentence. Shays eventually moved to New York, where he died.

CHAPTER FOUR

The Constitutional Convention

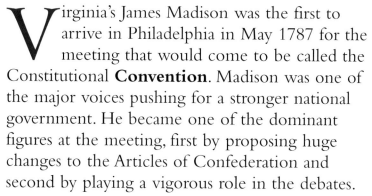

Virginia's James Madison was the first to arrive in Philadelphia in May 1787 for the meeting that would come to be called the Constitutional **Convention**. Madison was one of the major voices pushing for a stronger national government. He became one of the dominant figures at the meeting, first by proposing huge changes to the Articles of Confederation and second by playing a vigorous role in the debates.

The meeting took place in what is now called Independence Hall, in the same room where the Declaration of Independence had been debated and approved. The congress gave the Convention a clear goal: to meet "for the sole and express purpose of revising the Articles of Confederation."

This Great Council

"As the time approaches for opening the business of the federal convention, it is natural that every lover of his country should experience some anxiety. . . . Upon the event of this great council, indeed, depends every thing that can be essential to the dignity and stability of the national character."

Pennsylvania Packet, *a newspaper, May 11, 1787*

The Delegates

Fifty-five delegates attended the convention, although not all joined in every session. They came from all states except Rhode Island. (Its legislature objected to the idea of strengthening the national government.) New York did not have an official voice because two of the state's three delegates left the convention on July 10. Under the rules of the convention, the one New York delegate who remained—Alexander Hamilton—could not vote.

Many delegates had served in the Congress, and about half had served in the Continental army or the militia. Eight had signed the Declaration of Independence. About half were lawyers, while most of the others were businessmen or farmers. Some of the country's ablest leaders were not there. A few, such as Patrick Henry and Richard Henry Lee of Virginia, were absent because they opposed the idea of changes to the Articles. Others, such as John Adams and Thomas Jefferson, were busy elsewhere.

State leaders take a break from the convention in Philadelphia in 1787. At eighty-one years old, Benjamin Franklin (seated center left) was the eldest of the delegates at the Constitutional Convention.

Madison's Journal

The Constitutional Convention had an official secretary, but his notes were sketchy. Several delegates made notes of the proceedings that supplement this record. The most extensive notes were penned by James Madison. Each night, he copied his notes into a journal that provides a detailed look at the convention's delegates, debates, and decisions. Madison's notes have proved over time to be the most complete original record of the historic event.

First Decisions

The convention opened for business on May 15, 1787, with seven states—New York, New Jersey, Pennsylvania, Delaware, Virginia, North Carolina, and South Carolina—present. (Delegates from other states arrived later.) Those seven states unanimously chose George Washington to preside over the meeting. They also agreed that each state would have a single vote.

The Virginia Plan

A few days into the convention, Edmund Randolph of Virginia rose to offer some **resolutions** for the meeting to consider. They were, together, called the Virginia Plan and were largely the work of James Madison. Other Virginia delegates had agreed with Madison's plan.

The Virginia Plan represented a radical step—not a revision of the Articles of Confederation but their complete replacement. The proposed national government would have three branches—a legislature (which came to be called Congress), an **executive**, and a **judiciary**. The legislature would have two houses, and representation

At the Constitutional Convention, Edmund Randolph presented the Virginia Plan, the radical and historic proposal on which the Constitution of the United States was based. Randolph (left) was one of three delegates who ultimately refused to sign the final version of the Constitution.

in both would be based on state population. A council formed of the members of the executive branch and some judges would have the power to veto any laws passed by the legislature.

The plan was discussed for several days, and on May 30, a key vote was taken. In that vote, the delegates agreed that they would work to create a "national government . . . [with] a supreme legislative, executive, and judiciary." In other words, they were scrapping the Articles of Confederation and creating an entirely new government. They would lay down the basic structure and rules of this new government in a single document: the Constitution of the United States of America.

Working Out the Details

Over the next two weeks, the delegates debated the Virginia Plan. They decided to eliminate the council with veto power. They fixed the terms of office for the two houses of Congress.

A major sticking point, however, was the issue of representation in the legislature. States with larger populations liked the idea of proportionate representation—with more people, they would have more members. Small states objected to what would be a loss of power for them. After all, under the Articles of Confederation, each state had an equal vote in the Confederation Congress.

Power for the States

"It is easy to foresee that there will be much difficulty in organizing a government upon this great scale, and at the same time reserving to the state legislatures a sufficient portion of power for promoting and securing the prosperity and happiness of their respective citizens."

George Mason, delegate from Virginia, May 1787

Arguments about Representation

The debates about representation were often bitter. On July 5, the delegates agreed to a compromise. In the lower house (the House of Representatives), representation would be based on population; in the upper house (the Senate), there would be two members for each state, large or small.

The delegates still faced a major decision, however—how to measure the states' population in order to apportion seats in the lower house. Southern states wanted to count African American slaves in the population when allocating seats, even though slaves would not be allowed to vote. On July 16, the convention adopted another compromise. Slaves would be counted, but not person for person. Five slaves would count the same as three free people for the purpose of representation.

A Chief Executive

Other debates focused on the nature and power of the executive branch. Should it consist of one person or several? Who should choose this person or persons? What powers should he or they have?

These matters were resolved in September. The delegates agreed that a single chief executive—a president —would be elected by officials called electors, chosen by each state. States would have as many electors as they had members of the legislature. They also agreed to give the president a four-year term and the power to veto laws passed by the legislature. (Congress could override that veto, however, if two-thirds of the members of both houses voted against it.)

The Judiciary

The judiciary would be independent of both legislative and executive

The period of the convention during which the delegates hammered out the details of the Constitution is known as the "Great Debate." The discussion lasted from early August to mid-September 1787.

power. The job of the judiciary would be to settle disputes that arose under the laws created by the legislature and enforced by the executive branch. The judiciary would consist of the Supreme Court, the highest legal authority, and any other courts of law that Congress may choose to create to meet the nation's needs.

Checks and Balances

The result was a government with checks and balances, or one where legislative, executive, and judicial powers were in the hands of different people or groups. The legislature had the power to make laws, but the president could veto them. A president's veto could be overridden and, if that person abused the office by committing "high crimes and misdemeanors," he could be removed from office.

Slavery, Trade, and Taxes

Slavery arose as an issue once more. Southern states wanted to prevent laws banning the importing of slaves from abroad, a trade that many northern delegates opposed. Once more, the convention compromised. The final document said that no law banning foreign slave trade could be passed before 1808, but it did not remove the possibility of banning foreign slave trade after that date.

The Constitutional Convention gave Congress the right to raise taxes

Establishing a Constitution

"We the people of the United States, in order to form a more perfect union, establish justice, insure domestic tranquility, provide for the general defence, promote the general welfare, and secure the blessings of liberty to ourselves and our posterity, do ordain and establish this Constitution of the United States."

Preamble to the U.S. Constitution, 1787

and to control commerce between the states. It also agreed to what is called the "elastic clause," which gives Congress the authority "to make all laws which shall be necessary and proper." Congress has since used this power to pass a huge variety of laws.

Changes in the Future

A key decision involved how changes could be made to the Constitution in the future. The Articles of Confederation had required unanimous approval of any changes by both the Congress and the state legislatures. The delegates realized that one state could block all the others from acting. They decided that future changes, or amendments, could go into effect if approved by three-fourths of the states.

A Bill of Rights

Virginia's George Mason urged delegates to add a bill of rights—a statement of the individual rights that were guaranteed to each citizen. Others backed him. But most delegates feared that debating such a bill of rights would take too long. Weary after meeting for four months, they defeated Mason's motion.

Drafting the Document

From September 8 to 12, a committee of five members worked on putting the Constitution in final form. Much of this work was done by Gouverneur Morris of Pennsylvania. The next few days were spent making finishing touches to the work. On September 15, 1787, all eleven states that could vote approved the final document.

James Madison (1751–1836)

Born in Virginia, James Madison attended Princeton University in New Jersey. The Revolution began just a few years after he graduated, and he quickly joined the cause. Madison took part in Virginia's state government until joining the Congress in 1780. A fervent lover of Virginia, he also believed in strong national power.

After working to create and win approval of the Constitution, Madison served in the first House of Representatives. There, he helped write and win passage of the Bill of Rights. When the nation's leaders began to split into political factions, Madison allied himself with his close friend Thomas Jefferson. During Jefferson's eight years as president, Madison was secretary of state. He was then elected to two terms as president himself. After retiring, Madison worked on his journal of the Constitutional Convention, a valuable historic record.

These documents are the original first and last pages of the United States Constitution. The entire document is four pages long and is exhibited at the National Archives in Washington, D.C., alongside the Bill of Rights and the Declaration of Independence.

Two days later, the delegates gathered again to sign it. James Wilson of Pennsylvania gave a short speech written by Benjamin Franklin, who was too weak to speak himself. Franklin tried to convince all members to sign, but some refused to do so. In the end, thirty-nine delegates signed their names to the document.

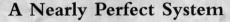

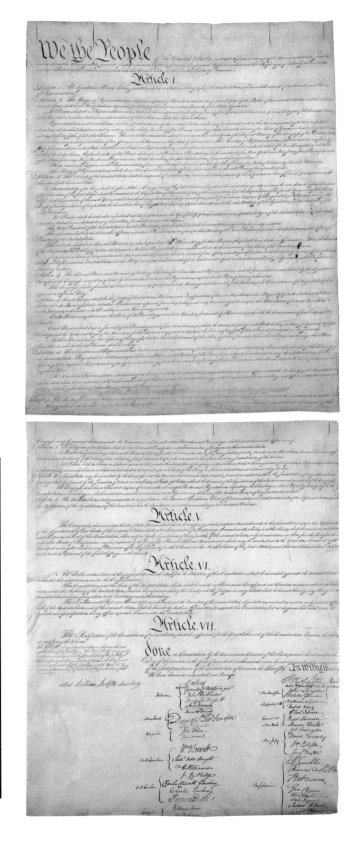

A Nearly Perfect System

"I confess that there are several parts of this Constitution which I do not at present approve, but I am not sure I shall never approve them. . . . It therefore astonishes me, sir, to find this system approaching so near to perfection as it does. . . . Thus I consent, sir, to this Constitution, because I expect no better, and because I am not sure, that it is not the best."

Benjamin Franklin,
September 17, 1787

CHAPTER FIVE

Ratifying the Constitution

The writing of the Constitution did not guarantee its acceptance. Objections voiced at the Constitutional Convention were repeated across the country as the people debated the new framework of government. In some states, the debate was quite heated.

The Congress Accepts the Constitution

The Constitution passed its first hurdle in the Congress. Some of its members strongly objected to the fact that the convention had gone beyond its aim of simply improving the Articles. They also attacked specific parts of the new framework for government. Still, many members of the Congress wanted a stronger national government, and they overcame the objections of others. They then sent the Constitution to the states for **ratification**.

The Approval Process

Delegates at the convention had worried that the state legislatures would never approve the document because their powers were being weakened. They wrote into the document, therefore, the condition that it had to be approved by special ratifying conventions in each state. This allowed them time to gather support. They also decided that only nine of the thirteen states needed to approve the Constitution for it to go into effect.

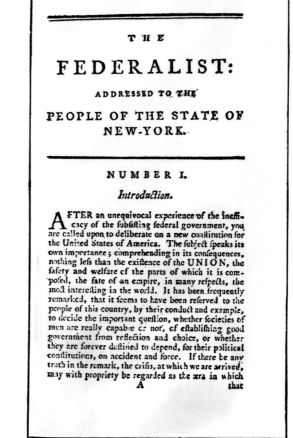

The Federalist Papers called for citizens to approve the Constitution on the grounds that a strong government would make the nation more stable and more just.

The Federalists

Those in favor of ratifying the new Constitution called themselves "Federalists." The Federalists made several points in favor of ratifying the Constitution. They said that the country desperately needed a national government with the power to tax and regulate trade. They said it needed an executive and judicial power and argued that the new government would give the country more security. Madison, Hamilton, and John Jay wrote a series of pamphlets called *The Federalist Papers* to try to convince people to favor the Constitution. The papers clearly spelled out the problems with the Articles and explained how the Constitution solved them.

Opposing the Constitution

The critics of the Constitution were known as "Antifederalists." These opponents formed a talented group that included old-time Patriots such

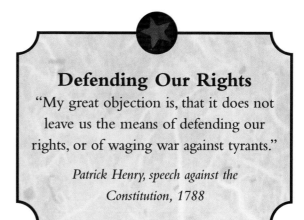

as John Hancock, Samuel Adams, and Patrick Henry, together with new political figures such as George Clinton, governor of New York. They argued against the new plan of government. The Antifederalists said that

Objections to the Constitution

One opponent of the Constitution voiced her objections in Massachusetts in 1788. Mercy Otis Warren, a playwright and historian, complained about the secrecy in which the Constitution had been produced—early on, delegates to the Constitutional Convention had agreed to keep their proceedings secret. Warren also had doubts about the content of the Constitution, and her comments reflected the doubts of many other people. The new national government, she said, would take away the power of individual states. Warren also objected to the lack of a bill

Mercy Otis Warren

of rights and heaped scorn on the idea that amendments to the Constitution, such as a bill of rights, could be added later: "The very suggestion, that we ought to trust to the precarious hope of amendments . . . after we have voluntarily fixed the shackles on our own necks should have awakened a double degree of caution."

the government of a republic should be small so that it would be close to the people. The Constitution, they claimed, would reduce the powers of the states and the people by making the national government stronger.

The Need for a Bill of Rights

The Antifederalists also complained about the lack of a bill of rights. They wanted the Constitution to contain a clear statement of people's rights that the government could not violate. Several states said that adding a bill of rights was a condition of their approving the Constitution.

Ratification

The Federalists moved quickly to win approval where they could. In little over two months, Federalists in Delaware organized a ratifying convention and gained their state's approval for the Constitution. The states of Pennsylvania, New Jersey, and Georgia quickly followed, as did Connecticut, Maryland, and South Carolina.

The first challenge came in Massachusetts, which had strong Antifederalist leaders. The Federalists convinced the ratifying convention there to approve the Constitution by pledging to approve a bill of rights as soon as the new government was formed. Even after that promise, the vote in Massachusetts was close—187 in favor and 168 against.

A Close Vote

With the approval of eight states, Federalists only needed one more. While fierce debates raged in Virginia and New York, New Hampshire voted in favor of the Constitution, although its convention wanted twelve amendments added to it. New Hampshire's vote meant the Constitution was ratified, but the Federalists wanted to win in both Virginia and New York, two of the largest states. Without the approval of those two states, they knew the new government would be weakened.

The debate opened in Virginia on June 2, 1788, and lasted almost the entire month. George Mason and Patrick Henry spoke forcefully against the document, but eventually Mason was won over by the promise to include a bill of rights. Late in June, the Virginia state convention approved the Constitution.

The Last States Ratify

When New York's convention opened, Antifederalists were in the majority. Playing for time, Hamilton got the meeting to postpone a vote until New Hampshire and Virginia had been heard from. While they waited, he and fellow Federalists worked on convincing some key

Patrick Henry (1736–1799)

Born in Virginia, Patrick Henry was not part of the wealthy planter aristocracy that dominated the colony's politics. He grew up in a frontier region and began working in a store at the age of fifteen. Henry worked for several years, bought his own farm, and married and had children. Then his farmhouse burned down, and, at age twenty-three, he took up law to have a way to earn money. Henry became famous during the protests against the Stamp Act of 1765, when he gave a stirring speech that persuaded Virginia's legislature to oppose the British law, which imposed taxes on the colonies.

Henry served briefly in the Continental Congress and also as governor of Virginia. He bitterly opposed the Constitution and campaigned for a bill of rights. Henry remained active in politics until the end of his life.

members to switch their votes. The news of Virginia's approval helped. Late in July, New York approved the Constitution, although only narrowly and with the recommendation that a bill of rights be added.

North Carolina withheld its approval until a bill of rights seemed sure of being created. In the fall of 1788, it, too, voted in favor of the new government. Rhode Island held out until May 1790.

A New Government

With the Constitution approved, the Confederation Congress began plans

The 1788 "Ship of State" parade in New York City honored Federalist Alexander Hamilton, who succeeded in persuading New Yorkers to approve the Constitution.

for its own termination and the sitting of a new government. It set January 7, 1789, as the date for the states to choose presidential electors and February 4 as the date for them to cast their votes. The new U.S. government would count those votes to discover who the first president would be. The Congress did not set dates for the election of members to the new legislature, but left it to the states.

No Government

The United States was actually without a government for several months in late 1788 and early 1789. On November 1, 1788, the Confederation Congress adjourned for the last time. Not until April 1, 1789, did the new House of Representatives officially meet. The Senate opened for business a few days later, but the first U.S. president was not sworn in until April 30.

CHAPTER SIX

The Government Starts Work

Delegates to the Constitutional Convention had worried a great deal about the new government they were creating. The new House of Representatives would be filled with members chosen by the people. Would voters make intelligent choices, or would they elect **demagogues** who threatened order? The delegates had also worried about the presidency. They feared putting too much power in the hands of one person. With the Constitution ratified, it was time to put the new framework of government to the test.

Electing Members

The Constitution had not mandated a specific day for states to elect members of Congress, and their selection took place over a period of several months. Some states voted for House members as early as September 30, 1788. Others voted several months later. Members of the Senate were chosen not by voters, but by state legislatures.

The two houses of Congress started work early in April 1789. On April 6, Congress counted the electoral votes for president. To no one's surprise, George Washington won unanimously. Messengers were dispatched to inform him and John Adams of Massachusetts, who was chosen as vice president.

Washington (center right) was inaugurated as the first U.S. president in 1789. He was an excellent first president and served two four-year terms.

The First President

Washington was reluctant to leave retirement to take on the burden of the presidency, but he felt it was his duty to do so. On April 30, 1789, on the porch of a new building in New York City called Federal Hall, he took the oath of office. Afterwards, Washington addressed the members of Congress. Speaking nervously, he asked for God's help in carrying out this new experiment in government.

Congress debated what the new chief executive should be called. Grand titles such as "His Majesty, the President" and "His Elective Highness" were suggested. Eventually, Congress settled on "President of the United States" and "Mr. President."

Congress in Action

Congress went right to work. Two early acts raised revenue by putting a **tariff** on imported goods and a tax on ships using U.S. ports. Then, in just three months—July through September of 1789—Congress filled out the structure of the federal government. It created three executive departments, the Department of State, the War Department, and the Treasury Department. The Judiciary Act created a federal court system that included thirteen district courts, three courts of

In 1791, the ten amendments that make up the Bill of Rights were finally ratified. Ever since, the Bill of Rights has been a guiding force in U.S. society.

appeal, and a Supreme Court above them all. The law gave the Supreme Court the right to hear appeals on cases decided in state courts. Finally, the Judiciary Act created the office of the attorney general, who would be the nation's chief legal officer.

The Bill of Rights

Congress approved several amendments to the Constitution, collectively called the Bill of Rights. The amendments were each voted on separately —twelve were approved, although, in the end, the states ratified only ten. These amendments guaranteed certain rights: free speech and press, freedom of religion, and freedom of **assembly**. They also said that all Americans had the right to a trial by jury. The last

The Census

The Constitution required that the government conduct a count of all people in the country every ten years. That population count, or census, would then be used to determine how many members each state would have in the House of Representatives. On March 1, 1790, Congress authorized the first census to take place. Remarkably, it was completed by August 1, even though the census workers had to travel long distances by horseback. Secretary of State Thomas Jefferson used U.S. marshals to carry out the counts. They counted just under 4 million people. Almost 700,000 of them—more than one in six—were African American slaves.

The First Amendment

"Congress shall make no law respecting an establishment of religion, or prohibiting the free exercise thereof; or abridging the freedom of speech, or of the press; or the right of the people peaceably to assemble, and to petition the government for a redress of grievances."

First Amendment to the Constitution, 1791

Washington's first cabinet members were (from left to right): Henry Knox, Thomas Jefferson, Alexander Hamilton, and Edmund Randolph.

amendment stated that all powers not specifically granted to the federal government in the Constitution belonged to the states.

Washington Sets Precedents

President Washington knew that his actions would serve as a model for future presidents. He acted carefully, therefore, to put the new government on a strong foundation.

Washington named able leaders to head the executive departments. He picked Thomas Jefferson as the first secretary of state; former war comrade Henry Knox as secretary of war; Alexander Hamilton as secretary of the Treasury; and fellow Virginian Edmund Randolph as attorney general. Washington met regularly with these department heads, who were known as the president's "cabinet."

The Constitution specified that the president should report regularly to Congress on the state of the nation. Washington sent reports each year, setting a precedent for the president's annual State of the Union address.

Washington wanted to leave office after one term, but he was persuaded to accept reelection in 1792. In 1797, however, he finally did retire. (In the 1950s, the Constitution was amended to limit presidents to serving a maximum of two terms, as Washington had done.)

Hamilton's Policies

In January of 1790, Hamilton reported to Congress on the country's financial credit. The nation owed more than $50 million, he said, about one-fifth of it in foreign loans. To address the problem, Hamilton set forth an ambitious plan. The federal government would create a fund to pay the interest on the nation's debt. It would also take on the states' debts.

Hamilton's plan involved devaluing some loan certificates held by people who had lent money to the government during the war. The proposal also called for the creation of new taxes to help pay for the increased national debt. For both these reasons, the plan received some opposition, especially to the idea of the federal government taking on the state's debts. Northern states liked it because they had the largest unpaid debts, but many states in the South, having taken care of their debts, opposed it.

Hamilton won approval when Jefferson suggested a compromise. The Constitution had referred to the creation of a federal district that would be home to a new U.S. capital. Hamilton agreed to locating the capital on the banks of the Potomac River, bordering the southern states, if the Southerners backed his financial plan.

Next, toward the end of 1790, Hamilton proposed creating a national bank. This also won passage, although Southerners were again not happy.

The Whiskey Rebellion

One of Hamilton's economic measures during his time as secretary of the Treasury led to a rebellion. In March 1791, Congress passed a tax on whiskey that had been urged by Hamilton. The tax hit western farmers hard because, when they grew extra grain, they turned it into whiskey that they could sell to make money. Now, they would have to pay a tax on the liquor. Farmers in western Pennsylvania rebelled in 1794 and marched in protest. Encouraged by Hamilton, Washington led thousands of Pennsylvania militiamen to the western part of the state. There was no fight, although some leaders were arrested. Still, the action showed that the new federal government would take steps to enforce the law.

As early as 1776, a committee was appointed by the Congress to design a seal, or official stamp, for the United States. This design by secretary of the Congress Charles Thomson was the one finally approved in 1782. The motto "E Pluribus Unum" means "Out of Many, One."

Divisions Grow

Finally, in late 1791, Hamilton proposed laws aimed at promoting the growth of manufacturing industries. Southerners, including Jefferson and Madison, grew increasingly unhappy with Hamilton's ideas. Adding to these differences were disagreements over developments in Europe. By the early 1790s, a revolution had overthrown the monarchy in France. France and Britain were at war again, and that war worsened the divisions in the United States. Jefferson supported France, while Hamilton favored Britain.

The Party System

By 1792, Jefferson and Hamilton were feuding, and their supporters were harshly criticizing each other. This split led to the formation of the country's first political factions (which would, in years to come, evolve into political parties). Hamilton's followers called themselves Federalists. They were strongest in the North and in middle states. Jefferson's supporters were the Democratic-Republicans. Their chief support was in the South and among small farmers.

Washington refused to serve as president for a third term. Old and tired, he was frustrated by the growing bitterness between the factions. In late 1796, he published a farewell address to the nation. In it, he warned the nation's leaders not to ally themselves with any foreign country. He also warned against the political divisions that were splitting the country.

A Warning Against Party Politics

"Let me . . . warn you in the most solemn manner against the baneful effects of the spirit of party. . . . It serves always to distract the public councils and enfeeble the public administration. It agitates the community with ill-founded jealousies and false alarms; kindles the animosity of one part against another; foments . . . riot and insurrection."

Washington's Farewell Address, 1796

Time Line

1774 September 5: First Continental Congress opens in Philadelphia.

1775 May 10: Second Continental Congress opens in Philadelphia.

1776 May 10: Congress advises colonies to write constitutions.
July 2: Congress votes in favor of independence.
Board of War is formed by Congress.

1777 November 15: Congress approves Articles of Confederation.

1781 March 2: Confederation Congress begins governing the nation.

1783 Treaty of Paris.

1785 May 8: Congress passes Land Ordinance of 1785.

1786 September 11–14: Annapolis conference discusses regulating trade and plans a meeting to consider reforms to Articles of Confederation.
September 26: Shays's Rebellion begins.

1787 May 25: Constitutional Convention opens in Philadelphia.
May 29: Edmund Randolph offers Virginia Plan.
July 13: Congress passes Northwest Ordinance.
September 17: U.S. Constitution is signed.
September 28: Congress sends Constitution to states for ratification.
October 27: First of *The Federalist Papers* is published.
December 7: Delaware is first state to ratify Constitution.

1788 June 21: New Hampshire ratifies Constitution, making it official.
June 25: Virginia ratifies Constitution.
July 26: New York ratifies Constitution.
November 1: Confederation Congress adjourns.

1789 February 4: Presidential electors vote in first presidential election.
April 1: House of Representatives meets in first official session.
April 5: Senate meets in first official session.
April 30: Washington is sworn in as president.
July 4: Congress puts tariffs on imported goods.
July 20: Congress passes Tonnage Act, taxing ships using U.S. ports.
September 24: Congress passes Judiciary Act.
September 25: Congress approves twelve amendments to Constitution (the Bill of Rights).

1790 January: Hamilton proposes plan to deal with national and state debts.
May 29: Rhode Island becomes thirteenth and last state to ratify Constitution.
July 10: Congress votes to build new national capital in southern Maryland.
December 14: Hamilton proposes creation of a national bank.

1791 December 5: Hamilton proposes laws to support growth of industry.

Glossary

assembly: bringing together a group of people.

bill of rights: statement of basic rights that must not be violated.

charter: official document granting rights and laying out laws and duties.

colony: settlement, area, or country owned or controlled by another nation.

congress: meeting. The name "Congress" was given to the first meetings of delegates from the British colonies and was then adopted as the name of the U.S. legislature when the United States formed a national government.

constitution: document that lays down the basic rules and laws of a nation or organization.

convention: large meeting. Political conventions bring together representatives to make decisions.

delegate: person chosen to represent a group at a meeting or in making decisions.

demagogue: leader who uses false claims to appeal to people and thereby gain power.

democracy: government system under which citizens can vote on decisions about how they are governed.

executive: having to do with carrying out the law and managing public affairs.

federal: national, or having to do with the whole nation rather than separate states.

frontier: edge of something known or settled. In the early years of the United States, the frontier meant the most westward point of white settlement.

imports: goods brought into a country.

judiciary: branch of government that interprets the law, settles disputes, and administers justice.

legislature: group of officials that makes laws.

militia: group of citizens organized into an army (as opposed to an army of professional soldiers, or regulars).

ordinance: law or regulation.

Patriot: American who supported the American Revolution; more generally, a person who is loyal to and proud of his or her country.

radical: involving or supporting huge changes in the way things are done.

ratification: official approval required before a proposed law or action can go into effect.

republic: nation that is led by elected officials and that has no monarch.

resolution: statement of principle by a legislative assembly.

speculator: person who buys land or other assets, hoping to sell later at a profit.

tariff: tax on imported goods.

tax: sum charged by the government on purchases, property ownership, or income and used to pay for public services or the cost of governing.

territory: geographical area belonging to the United States but not part of any state.

treaty: agreement made after negotiations among two or more nations or groups.

unanimous: agreed by everyone.

veto: use official power to stop something becoming law.

Further Resources

Books

Burgan, Michael. *John Adams: Second U.S. President* (Revolutionary War Leaders). Chelsea House, 2000.

Hakim, Joy. *The New Nation* (A History of US volume 4). Oxford University Press, 2002.

Leebrick, Kristal. *The United States Constitution* (Let Freedom Ring: the American Revolution). Capstone, 2002.

Schmittroth, Linda. *American Revolution Primary Sources* (American Revolution Reference Library). UXL, 2000.

Stein, R. Conrad. *The Declaration of Independence* (Cornerstones of Freedom). Children's Press, 1995.

Places to Visit

National Archives and Records Administration
700 Constitution Avenue, NW
Washington, DC 20408
Telephone: (866) 272-6272

Web Sites

The Constitution for Kids
www.usconstitution.net/constkids4.html
Web site devoted to explaining the U.S. Constitution and its amendments to all age groups—this page is specifically aimed at 4th to 8th grade.

Library of Congress - Thomas
thomas.loc.gov/
The Library of Congress offers legislative information, including information about how Congress makes laws, and links to Congressional offices and historical documents.

NARA/The National Archives Experience: The Charters of Freedom
www.archives.gov/national_archives_ experience/charters/charters.html
The National Archives web site displays images of the United States' most important historical documents.

The White House: Government
www.whitehouse.gov/government/
White House web site explains the role of the executive office and provides links to government departments and offices.

Index